ONE IGUANA TWO IGUANAS

A Story of Accident, Natural Selection, and Evolution

SNEED B. COLLARD III

TILBURY HOUSE PUBLISHERS, THOMASTON, MAINE

For Jack Grove, scientist, teacher, friend. —Sneed

Tilbury House Publishers
12 Starr St.
Thomaston, Maine 04861
800–582–1899 • www.tilburyhouse.com

First edition: December 2018 • 10 9 8 7 6 5 4 3 2 1

Library of Congress Control Number: 2018956504

Cover and interior design by Frame25 Productions
Printed in the United States via Four Colour Print Group

Photo Credits

Front cover, title page, and page 3 photos, Sneed B. Collard III · pages 4 – 5, Jack Grove / www.JSGrove.com · p.6, Jack Grove / www.JSGrove.com · p.7, Gudkov Andrey / Shutterstock · p.8, Jack Grove / www.JSGrove.com · p.9 top, Leonard Lee Rue III / Science Source · p.9 bottom (map), Peter Hermes Furian / Shutterstock · p.10, Sneed B. Collard III · p.11 top, Jack Grove / www.JSGrove.com · p.11 bottom, Gavin Morrison / Shutterstock · p.12, Sneed B. Collard III · p.13 top, pilesasmiles / iStock · p.13 inset, Ralph Lee Hopkins / Science Source · p. 14, Jason Wells / Shutterstock · p.15, luisrock62 / iStock · p.16, Sneed B. Collard III · p.17 top, Gudkov Andrey / Shutterstock · p.17 inset, Sneed B. Collard III · p.18, Sneed B. Collard III · p.19 top, Sneed B. Collard III · p.19 sidebar, U.S. Department of Energy · p.20, Jack Grove / www.JSGrove.com · p.22 main, buteo / Shutterstock · p.22 inset, Gail Johnson / Shutterstock · p.23 sidebar, from "Hybridization masks speciation in the evolutionary history of the Galápagos marine iguana," by Amy MacLeod, Ariel Rodríguez, Miguel Vences, Pablo Orozco-terWengel, Carolina García, Fritz Trillmich, Gabriele Gentile, Adalgisa Caccone, Galo Quezada, Sebastian Steinfartz, published in Proc. R. Soc. B 2015 282 20150425; DOI: 10.1098/rspb.2015.0425 (3 June 2015) · pages 24 – 25, USO / iStock · p.25 inset, Jack Grove / www.JSGrove.com · p.26, Sneed B. Collard III · p.27 top, Steve Cymro, Shutterstock · p.27 inset, Jack Grove / www.JSGrove.com · p.28, Fotos593 / Shutterstock · p.28 inset, Sneed B. Collard III · p.29 top, Mindstorm / Shutterstock · p.29 sidebar, Steve Cymro / Shutterstock · p.30 main and inset photos, Sneed B. Collard III · p.31 sidebar photos, Sneed B. Collard III · p.32, Eachat / iStock · p.33, USO / iStock · p.34, Paul D. Stewart / Science Source · p.35 sidebar images, The Natural History Museum, London / Science Source · pages 36 – 37, Sneed B. Collard III · p.38, Jack Grove / www.JSGrove.com · p.39 top, Sneed B. Collard III · p.39 bottom, reisegraf.ch / Shutterstock · back cover main, buteo / Shutterstock · back cover inset, Jack Grove / www.JSGrove.com

ONE IGUANA

Six hundred miles (1,000 km) off the coast of South America, almost exactly on Earth's equator, a charcoal-colored lizard sits on a shore of jagged lava rocks. The lizard is a marine iguana, and with its dark skin and bumpy head, it looks like it could have been carved from lava itself.

The iguana stretches two feet (0.6 meters) long from its snout to the tip of its tail. It soaks up intense tropical sunlight streaming down from the sky. Suddenly, though, it stands and walks to the water's edge. Without a glance, it does something no other lizard on earth does.

It dives beneath the ocean
surface to graze on plants!

TWO IGUANAS

A Galápagos land iguana eating a prickly pear cactus.

Nearby sits another kind of lizard, a land iguana, guarding a prickly pear cactus. The land iguana couldn't seem more different from the marine iguana.

It is more than twice as large. It has yellow skin. It eats different foods and lives in sandy underground burrows—not on the rocky shore. But here is the surprise.

As different as they are, the two iguanas are cousins. They are descended from the same ancestor who lived only a few million years ago—a mere blink of an eye in the history of life on Earth.

How did these two animals get to be so different? And how did they come to exist on this remote island in the vast Pacific?

The answers to these questions make a remarkable story.

BARREN
BEGINNINGS

The two iguanas live in the Galápagos Islands, which were formed by volcanoes thrusting up from the deep ocean floor. The oldest island roared and shoved its way above the ocean surface as long as 15 million years ago. It was barren of life.

But that would quickly change.

A volcanic eruption on Fernandina Island in 2018. Fernandina is one of the most recently formed islands in the Galápagos archipelago, and its volcano is still active.

The cinder cone of a volcano on Bartolomé Island, Galápagos.

UNITED STATES

Bermuda
(U.K.)

THE BAHAMAS

MEXICO

Turks and
Caicos Islands
(U.K.)

CUBA

Puerto Rico
(U.S.)

Anguilla
(U.K.)

Cayman Islands
(U.K.)

HAITI

Virgin
Islands

ANTIGUA &
BARBUDA

ST. KITTS
AND NEVIS

DOMINICAN
REPUBLIC

JAMAICA

Guadeloupe
(FRANCE)

BELIZE

DOMINICA

Martinique
(FRANCE)

HONDURAS

ST. VINCENT AND
THE GRENADINES

ST. LUCIA

BARBADOS

GUATEMALA

Aruba
(NETH.)

Curaçao
(NETH.)

GRENADA

EL SALVADOR

NICARAGUA

TRINIDAD AND
TOBAGO

COSTA RICA

PANAMA

VENEZUELA

GUYANA

*The Galápagos Islands
sit at the bottom of this
map, far offshore from
South America.*

COLOMBIA

SUR.

Galapagos Islands
(ECUADOR)

ECUADOR

BRAZIL

PERU

0 300 km
0 300 mi

EARLY ARRIVALS

Within months—maybe days—
seeds of plants arrived, carried
on winds from South and Central America. The seeds landed
in a rocky, hot environment
where very little rain fell. Most
of the seeds perished, but a
few lucky ones took hold, and
plants began to grow.

*A red-footed booby on
San Cristóbal Island.*

Sea lions in the Galápagos.

Along with the seeds, flying insects arrived. Like the seeds, most died. But with their tough outer shells, a few insects managed to survive and even reproduce.

It wasn't long before seabirds began visiting the island. Gulls, cormorants, boobies, and frigatebirds fed from the sea, but on the island they found a safe place, free from predators, to raise their young. Their droppings helped enrich the rocky volcanic soils. So did the poop of sea lions

A blue-footed booby diving for fish.

that hauled themselves ashore to rest. The nutrients from this "fertilizer" helped other plants and animals survive.

SOMETHING MISSING

Over the next few million years, additional islands rose from the ocean floor. They formed an island group, or archipelago.

Brown pelican in flight, Galápagos Islands.

Once in a while, older islands sank back below the sea surface, but newer islands roared up to replace them.

All this time, plants continued to arrive in the Galápagos. Some were carried by wind or floated on ocean currents. Others arrived as seeds in the poop of birds.

Flamingos and mangrove trees in the Galápagos.

A palo santo forest on Floreana Island, Galápagos, during the dry season.

Along the shores, mangrove trees grew. Farther inland, ghostly forests of palo verde and palo santo trees carpeted the flanks of volcanos.

Something was still missing, though: large land animals.

Sitting hundreds of miles from the nearest continent, the Galápagos Islands were just too far away. Any land animal that set out swimming or floating from South or Central America drowned, or starved, or missed the islands altogether. But then a lucky accident happened.

THE ACCIDENTAL ANCESTOR

A black ctenosaur in Costa Rica.

One day a raft of driftwood tumbled ashore in the surf. Weeks earlier, the wood had washed into the sea during a ferocious storm over Central America. Currents carried the raft hundreds of miles across open waters until, quite by accident, it landed on a Galápagos beach. Over the years, thousands of other sticks and logs had drifted to the Galápagos, but this raft was special.

This raft carried a passenger.

The passenger was a large ctenosaur (TEE-no-sore) lizard that had made its home in the coastal forests of Central America. During the storm it had been washed into a flooding river. The lizard saved itself by crawling up onto the stick raft as it was swept out to sea.

Most other animals would have died on the raft, but the ctenosaur was tough. It could survive months without eating and weeks without drinking. When it finally reached the Galápagos, it scampered off the raft and began nibbling on the plants that it found growing there. This lizard also carried a special cargo.

A ctenosaur as it might have looked when scrambling ashore in the Galápagos millions of years ago.

THE MATRIARCH

Eggs!

The lizard was a pregnant female. She scratched out a nest, laid her eggs, and buried them in the sand.

Soon, two dozen baby ctenosaur lizards hatched and explored in all directions. Several were eaten by crabs.

Others were eaten by gulls and frigatebirds. But some babies survived and grew.

Frigatebirds, like this one in the Galápagos Islands, have a wingspan up to 7.5 feet (2.3 meters) and can soar for weeks at a time without landing.

After a few years, they mated and began hatching babies of their own. With few predators and plenty of plants to eat, the lizards thrived. Some even swam or drifted to other Galápagos islands nearby.

A Sally Lightfoot crab in the Galápagos.

Male frigatebirds in courtship display.

HOW DO WE KNOW THIS?

We will never be sure how the first lizard arrived in the Galápagos, but we have solid indirect evidence for how it *may* have happened. DNA tests show that Galápagos iguanas are *most* closely related to ctenosaur lizards—lizards that live mostly in Central America and Mexico. This tells us that the Galápagos iguana ancestor probably came from Central America, more than 900 miles (1,500 km) away. How did it reach the Galápagos? Ctenosaur lizards are strong swimmers, but it's doubtful that one could survive in the water for the many days or weeks it would take to make such a long journey. Instead, many scientists believe that the lizard floated on a raft of logs or other debris and was carried to the Galápagos by ocean currents. To colonize the islands, of course, the lizard had to have been an egg-bearing female—or been joined by at least one other ctenosaur "castaway" of the opposite sex.

NATURAL SELECTION

But the lizards did not stay the same in their new home.

The harsh Galápagos environment hammered and molded them into a new species, or kind of animal. How? Through a process called *natural selection*.

How did it work?

As in most other species, each lizard was slightly different from all the others. Some were bigger, some were smaller. Some could survive longer without water. Some could digest the local plants better than others could. Over time, those lizards that survived best in their new home stayed healthier and lived longer. Because of that, they had more babies and passed their better survival traits to their offspring.

A prickly pear cactus in the Galápagos.

Lava rock in the Galápagos.

WHY ARE INDIVIDUALS DIFFERENT?

In general, no two lizards are exactly alike. No two people or beetles or fish are exactly alike either. Why not? One big reason is that each of us grows and develops according to a set of instructions called _genes_. Genes are part of our _DNA_—the special material inside our cells that controls most of what we are and do. Human DNA, for instance, contains about 30,000 different genes. These genes help determine how we grow, what we look like, how sharp our eyesight is, how intelligent we are, how we behave—and thousands of other things that make us who we are.

But here's the thing: genes come in different forms called _alleles_. For instance, one allele of a gene might give a dog black hair, while another allele might give it red hair. What's more, in most kinds of living things, no two individuals have the same _combination_ of alleles. That makes each of us different. It also gives each of us advantages and disadvantages in different habitats or situations.

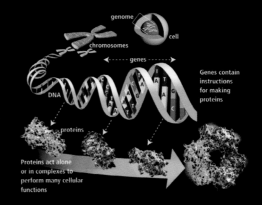

Human cells contain 23 pairs of chromosomes, or DNA molecules, each of which carries up to 2,000 genes.

RISE OF THE LAND IGUANAS

Over many, many generations, natural selection repeated itself again and again.

With each new batch of baby lizards, nature weeded out those that were not fit enough to survive. The survivors, though, mated and reproduced. They passed on their better features, or traits, to the next generation.

In time, the original lizard species changed, or evolved, into a brand-new species, a Galápagos land iguana. This new species was highly adapted to the Galápagos environment. It sheltered in underground burrows that protected it from extreme temperatures and hungry birds of prey. It moved slowly to conserve energy.

It developed a digestive system that allowed it to eat a variety of local plant leaves and fruits—even those of the islands' prickly pear cactuses. From these plants and fruits, the lizard obtained both the food and the water that it needed.

As land iguanas spread throughout the Galápagos, they encountered different conditions in different places. Each local environment shaped the lizards in various ways. Over time, there wasn't just one kind of Galápagos land iguana—there were several, three of which exist today.

INTO THE SEA

But the processes of natural selection and evolution had only just begun, and somewhere along the way, about four-and-a-half million years ago, a truly remarkable transformation took place. One group of iguanas began feeding in the sea!

USING DNA TO LEARN WHEN SPECIES SPLIT

Many people wonder how scientists can tell how long ago one species split off from another. Until recently, scientists had to rely on comparing fossils and the rocks they were found in. Unfortunately, not all animals leave a good fossil record, so this method doesn't always work. Scientists also compare the bodies of one species to another—but this method can be misleading, since major physical changes can happen very quickly.

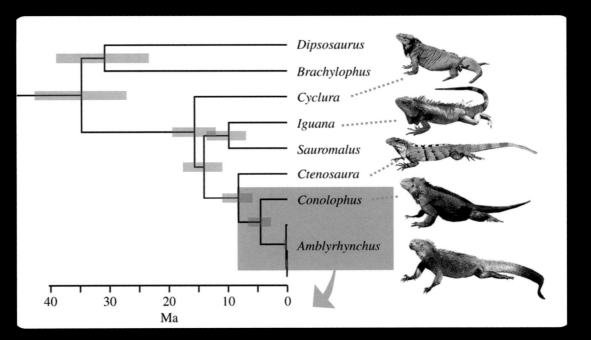

An iguana family tree suggests that Galápagos iguanas evolved from the ctenosaurs 8.25 million years ago, and the marine iguana (Amblyrhynchus cristatus) diverged from the land iguana (Conolophus sp) about 4.5 million years ago.

Recently, however, scientists have come up with a better dating tool: the DNA inside our cells. Scientists discovered that certain sections of our DNA seem to change at a predictable rate, like a clock. Scientists can compare this "time-keeping DNA" in two related species—and see how different the sections of DNA have become. That information, combined with fossil data, gives scientists a good idea how long ago two species separated from each other.

No one will ever be sure how it happened. Perhaps one year, on one island, a drought killed most of the land plants. Desperate for food, one or two land iguanas began eating the leafy green plants—the algae—exposed at low tide. While other land iguanas starved, these lizards survived.

They even reproduced, and their babies also ate green algae.

Natural selection favored the lizards that could digest the algae the best. Those lizards survived better on this new food source, and they passed this ability to their young. But evolution did not stop there.

Over time, some of the algae-eating iguanas made a discovery: An enormous "salad bowl" of algae grew beneath the sea surface!

EARTH'S ONLY MARINE LIZARD EVOLVES

Not all of the iguanas could reach the underwater algae, but some iguanas were naturally bigger or better swimmers.

The Galápagos marine iguana, Amblyrhynchus cristatus.

They could stay underwater longer and withstand the ocean's cool temperatures. Those iguanas survived better than the other iguanas, and once again, they passed their better features and abilities to their babies.

Through many, many generations, natural selection created
another new species.

Today's Galápagos marine iguana
has a flat tail for better swimming.
It has long, strong claws that allow
it to cling to rocks, even in surging
currents or waves. While underwater, it
conserves heat by restricting blood
flow to its skin.

A dried marine iguana head showing its
special "three-point," or tricuspid, teeth
for scraping algae from the sea bottom.

On land, its dark skin absorbs more warmth from the sun, allowing it to heat up
quickly after it has been in the chilly Galápagos waters.

It even has a gland in its nose that removes the extra ocean salt that the lizard
swallows while feeding.

The final result is a new animal that is almost perfectly adapted to its habitat and way of life. Of the more than 6,000 species of lizards on earth, the Galápagos marine iguana is the *only* one capable of diving into the ocean to graze on plants.

A marine iguana colony.

MEET THE INCREDIBLE SHRINKING IGUANA!

Every few years, warm waters replace the cooler waters surrounding the Galápagos. Scientists refer to this event as El Niño, and it is bad news for marine iguanas. Why? Because the leafy green algae that they eat dies, and many iguanas starve to death. A few years ago, however, scientists made a remarkable discovery. They found that when food is scarce, marine iguanas can actually *shrink*! Their skeletons can grow shorter by as much as twenty percent. These smaller animals require less food and have a better chance to survive El Niño. When cool waters—and food—return, the iguanas "regrow" to their original sizes. So far, marine iguanas are the only land vertebrates on earth that have been observed to do this, and it is yet another way these remarkable lizards have adapted to life in their harsh environment.

A LABORATORY OF
LIFE

The Galápagos marine and land iguanas are not the only land animals that the Galápagos islands have shaped.

A Galápagos finch.

One of the four Galápagos mockingbird species descended from a common ancestor.

Over the past millions of years, finches, mockingbirds, tortoises, and many other species accidentally flew, floated, or were carried to the Galápagos. Over time, they spread throughout the islands, and local habitats shaped these animals through the process of natural selection. In many cases, the animals evolved into entirely new species.

THE GALÁPAGOS ISLANDS' FAMOUS TORTOISES

The giant tortoises of the Galápagos are even more famous than the Galápagos iguanas. Up to fifteen species of tortoises once lived in the Galápagos. They all evolved from the same ancestor—a tortoise that floated or swam from South America millions of years ago. The different habitats of the Galápagos shaped the original tortoise species through natural selection. Some tortoises evolved to be bigger, some smaller. Those with rounded shells feed on plants closer to the ground. Those with "saddle-back" shells and longer necks reach taller plants. Humans, when they arrived, began collecting the tortoises for food, and several species became extinct. Today, the eleven remaining species are carefully protected throughout the islands.

A THEORY TAKES SHAPE

Darwin's Arch, off Darwin Island in the Galápagos.

Not surprisingly, it was the animals and plants of the Galápagos that helped the famous scientist Charles Darwin figure out how new species form.

The islands are located far from other land masses and are home to far fewer kinds of plants and animals than most other places. Many Galápagos species also are very different from species found elsewhere. All these factors make them an ideal place to think about the creation of new species.

As a young man, Darwin visited the Galápagos and studied the finches, tortoises, and other animals he found there.

He realized that each species is shaped by the environment and events where it lives. Darwin used the phrase *natural selection* to describe this process.

Today we know that natural selection has shaped and created every living thing on earth, and it is still at work. Scientists all over the world watch natural selection occur in many habitats and with many different living things.

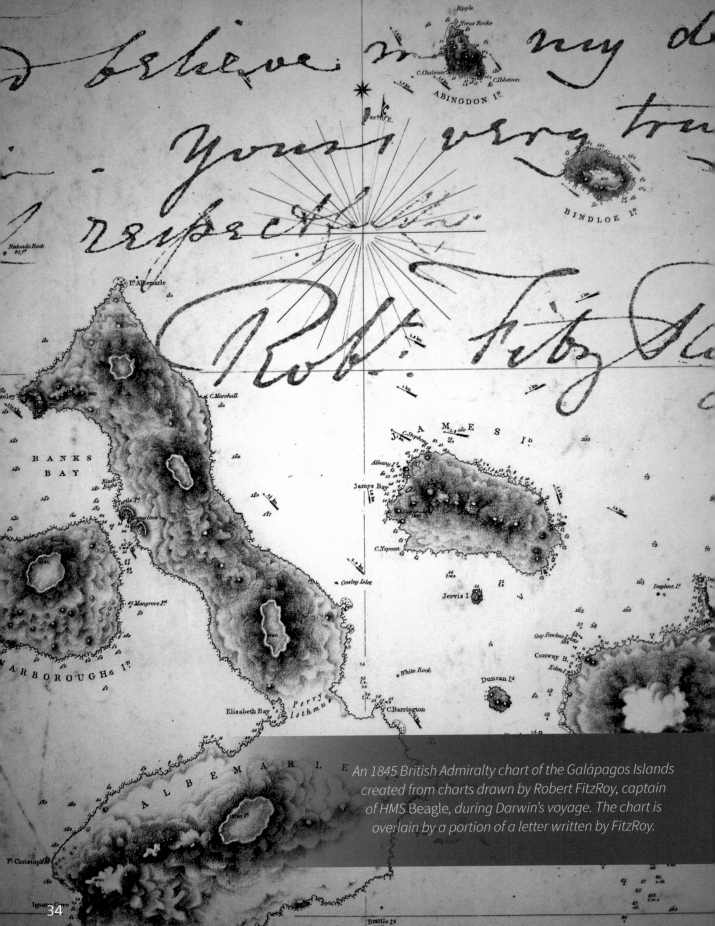

An 1845 British Admiralty chart of the Galápagos Islands created from charts drawn by Robert FitzRoy, captain of HMS Beagle, during Darwin's voyage. The chart is overlain by a portion of a letter written by FitzRoy.

Natural selection *can* take place in only one or two generations, but often it occurs over long periods of time. Observing it takes patience and hard work. Fast or slow, natural selection is happening around us *now*—even while, somewhere far from the South American mainland, a charcoal-colored lizard dives into the ocean for its next meal.

THE MAN WHO SAILED TO SEE

In 1831, when he was only twenty-two years old, Charles Darwin set out on a five-year voyage aboard a ship called the *Beagle*. His mission? To learn as much as possible about, well, *everything!* In the early 1800s, one big question scientists were asking themselves was how new species are made. By this time, people were digging up fossils that proved that many species had appeared—and disappeared—during Earth's history. But how? During his voyage, Darwin collected hundreds of animal specimens and shipped them home to England. When he returned from his voyage, he began thinking especially about all the species of finches he had collected from the Galápagos. Many looked the same, but there were small differences,

The differences among finches from different Galápagos islands—including the common cactus finch (left) and the large ground finch (right)—helped Charles Darwin form his theory of natural selection.

especially in their beaks. Their different beak shapes and sizes allowed them to feed on different kinds of seeds. Over the next twenty or so years, Darwin developed his thoughts and came up with the idea that natural selection creates new species.

Darwin wasn't the only scientist to discover how species are made. Another, Alfred Russel Wallace, came up with similar ideas at the same time. Today, both men get credit for changing how we think about the world and its living things.

Words and Phrases

adapt: to change in a way that helps one survive; this can happen through natural selection and evolution, or by changes in an organism's behavior or, in the case of the "incredible shrinking marine iguana," its body

algae: plants that grow underwater

allele: one form of a gene that controls something; for example, one allele may make a dandelion flower grow taller while a different allele may make the flower grow shorter

ancestor: a relative in the direct line that came before another living thing; for example your great-great-grandmother is one of your ancestors

archipelago: a group of islands

DNA: a kind of material inside living cells that holds instructions for how a living thing grows, functions, and behaves

El Niño: an event in which east to west trade winds weaken across the Pacific Ocean, causing warmer waters to pile up in the eastern Pacific Ocean

environment: the sum of our surroundings including the soil, climate, air, geography, and other living things

extinct: a word that describes a species that can no longer be found living anywhere on earth

evolve: to change; especially the process that describes the change in a kind of living thing over many generations

evolution: the process by which species change over time, often into entirely new species

fossils: bones, footprints, or other traces of a living thing that have been preserved and left behind

gene: a particular section of DNA that controls a certain thing; height or eye color, for instance

mangroves: certain kinds of plants that can live in places that are flooded with salt water

natural selection: the process by which nature "chooses" features that help a species survive; individuals with more useful features survive better, producing more offspring with those same traits or features. Over time, this leads to species that are better adapted to their environment.

nutrients: substances such as nitrogen and phosphorous that living things need to grow and stay healthy

perish(ed): die or disappear

predators: animals that survive by eating other animals

reproduce: to create babies or offspring

species: a group of living things that is very closely related; individuals usually only cooperate and breed with members of their own species. Examples of species include humans, dogs, American robins, blue whales, and so on.

Learning More About Evolution, Darwin, and the Galápagos

Considering how important evolution is to the history of the earth, it's surprising how few books for young people have been written about it. Here are a few solid titles to check out:

• *Billions of Years, Amazing Changes* by Laurence Pringle, Boyds Mills press, 2011.

• *Life on Earth: The Story of Evolution* by Steve Jenkins, Houghton Mifflin Harcourt, 2002.

• *Evolution: How We and All Living Things Came to Be* by Daniel Loxton, KidsCan Press, 2010.

• *Beastly Brains: Exploring How Animals Think, Talk, and Feel* by Nancy Castaldo, Houghton Mifflin Harcourt, 2017.

More information about Charles Darwin can be found in:

• *Charles and Emma: the Darwins' Leap of Faith*, by Deborah Heiligman, Henry Holt, 2009.

• *Who Was Charles Darwin?* by Deborah Hopkinson, Grosset & Dunlap, 2005.

• *Darwin and Evolution for Kids* by Kristan Lawson, Chicago Review Press, 2003.

A marine iguana with lava lizard hitchhiker.

Children's books about the Galápagos are even harder to find than those about evolution, but try:

• *Island: A Story of the Galápagos* by Jason Chin, Roaring Brook Press, 2012.

• *Where Are the Galapagos Islands?* by Megan Stine, Penguin Workshop, 2017.

To learn more about the animals and conservation in the Galaápagos, also take a look at the the website of the The Galápagos Conservancy (www.galapagos.org). And I highly recommend the short films about the Galápagos—including one featuring both kinds of iguanas—linked at the UNESCO page whc.unesco.org/en/list/1/video.

Author's Note

The information in this book comes from the best knowledge that scientists have discovered and collected about natural selection, evolution, and adaptation. Of

course, I had to imagine a few things. As I explain on page 17, no one knows *exactly* how the first ctenosaur lizard arrived in the Galápagos. Riding on driftwood seems a likely possibility, but the lizard might have reached the islands simply by swimming or riding ocean currents, too. What's important is that the lizard *did* reach the Galápagos, allowing natural selection to turn it into the various Galápagos iguanas that we enjoy and appreciate today.

No book like this evolves without the help of other people. First, I am indebted to my high school biology teacher, Len Miller, for clearly explaining evolution to me. I also am grateful to Dr. Jack Grove for first introducing me to the Galápagos and inspiring me to write about them. Several of Jack's wonderful photos appear in this book. Thank you, Walter and Carol Ratzlaf, for taking me to these amazing

islands, and to my family—Amy, Braden, and Tessa—for making the journey the adventure of a lifetime. Also, thanks to Vanessa Gallo for answering my questions about the Galápagos animals and El Niño. Huge credit is due to Dr. Amy MacLeod and her colleagues for their outstanding work on the evolution

of the Galápagos marine iguana, and for Dr. MacLeod's careful and thorough reading of my manuscript. I also owe thanks to University of Montana professor Scott Mills for reviewing and suggesting additions to the book. Finally, I'd like to thank Jonathan Eaton at Tilbury House Publishers for having the courage and conviction to publish a story that truly educates young people about their world.

About the Author

SNEED B. COLLARD III has evolved through several life stages. After graduating with honors in marine biology from U.C. Berkeley, he earned a master's degree in scientific instrumentation. Since then he has written more than 80 award-winning books for children and adults, including *Catching Air: Taking the Leap with Gliding Animals* and *Woodpeckers: Drilling Holes and Bagging Bugs*. To learn more about Sneed or set up an author visit or writing workshop, visit his website, www.sneedbcollardiii.com. And check out the weekly birding blog he writes with his son, Braden, at FatherSonBirding.com.

HOW NATURE WORKS

HOW NATURE WORKS books don't just catalog the natural world in beautiful photographs. They seek to understand why nature functions as it does. They ask questions, and they encourage readers to ask more. They explore nature's mysteries, sharing what we know and celebrating what we have yet to discover. Other HOW NATURE WORKS books include:

Catching Air:
Taking the Leap with Gliding Animals
Sneed B. Collard III
978-0-8848-496-7

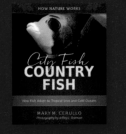

City Fish, Country Fish:
How Fish Adapt to Tropical Seas and Cold Oceans
Mary M. Cerullo
978-0-88448-529-2

Extreme Survivors:
Animals That Time Forgot
Kimberly Ridley
978-0-88448-500-1

Don't Mess with Me:
The Strange Lives of Venemous Sea Creatures
Paul Erickson
978-0-88448-551-3